STORIES OF
OUR AMERICAN
PATRIOTIC SONGS

Stories of Our
AMERICAN
Patriotic Songs

BY DR. JOHN HENRY LYONS

FORMER DIRECTOR OF MUSIC EDUCATION, PASADENA CITY SCHOOLS

ILLUSTRATED BY

JACOB LANDAU

THE VANGUARD PRESS, INC. NEW YORK

COPYRIGHT, 1940 AND 1942, BY JOHN HENRY LYONS

No portion of this book may be reprinted in any form without the written permission of the publisher, except by a reviewer who wishes to quote brief passages in connection with a review for a newspaper or magazine

Published simultaneously in Canada by the Copp Clark Publishing Company, Ltd., Toronto

Library of Congress Catalogue Card Number: 42-24375

The publisher and author wish to thank the following for their kind permission to use the musical arrangements of the songs in this book. The arrangements of "America," and "America, The Beautiful" are used by special permission of the Silver, Burdett Company of New York; those of "Maryland, My Maryland" and "Hail, Columbia," through the courtesy of the Cable Piano Company of Chicago; "Columbia, The Gem of the Ocean" and "Dixie," through the courtesy of the Rodeheaver Hall-Mack Company of Winona Lake, Indiana; "The Battle Cry of Freedom," "Yankee Doodle," and "The Battle Hymn of the Republic," through the courtesy of C. C. Birchard and Company of Boston. The arrangement of "The Star-Spangled Banner" is the Service Version, in the lower key just adopted by the 1942 National Anthem Committee.

MANUFACTURED IN THE UNITED STATES OF AMERICA

Contents

Dear Young Americans:

Today, more than ever, we are proud to be citizens of the United States, the largest and grandest of all Republics.

We are proud, too, of the great American songs of patriotism and freedom which have sung themselves into our hearts. The spirit of America is found in every line of these poems.

Knowing the origin of our familiar songs of patriotism may give them a new and deeper interest, and afford us a better understanding of the triumphant history of our glorious Republic—and of the meaning of our hard-won liberty.

Sincerely,

John Henry Lyons

August 1, 1942
Pasadena, California

The Star-Spangled Banner

It was the late summer of 1814. For more than two weary years the war of 1812 had been raging between the new republic of the United States of America and England, the former mother country.

The city of Washington had been under attack by the British. The new Capitol had been burned to the ground, and other buildings had been blazing for days. Even the President's home had been set on fire. But fortunately the fire had been put out in time. The walls of the house were easily repaired, and a heavy coat of white paint soon covered the damage. Ever since, the President's mansion, painted white from that time to this, has been known as the White House.

Toward the middle of September, the British were preparing to move against Baltimore. But first they had to destroy Fort McHenry, which guarded the city. It was to accomplish this that the largest and strongest ships in the British fleet sailed up Chesapeake Bay and anchored opposite the Fort.

Aboard the Admiral's flagship the British held a distinguished prisoner of war. Dr. William Beanes, a physician who came from the town of Upper Marlborough, Maryland, had been captured, and his friends feared for his safety. One of them, Francis Scott Key, a young Baltimore lawyer, determined to rescue the doctor. On September 13, 1814, armed with official papers from President Madison, Mr. Key set out with another friend, Mr. John Skinner, on the dangerous mission.

In a small government boat, under a flag of truce, the two men made their way across Chesapeake Bay to where the Admiral's ship was anchored. They reached the flagship, were courteously received, and were allowed to go on board. Mr. Key presented the Admiral with the official papers given him by President Madison, which stated that the doctor was not a soldier, but a private citizen, and therefore should be released. Also in Dr. Beanes' favor was the fact that he had once entertained at his home British officers of the flagship and had skillfully treated some of their wounded comrades.

Having considered the facts, the Admiral agreed to release Dr. Beanes. But unfortunately, as luck would have it, the British fleet was ready to open fire on Fort

McHenry with all their heavy guns at that very moment.

The Admiral felt sure of a speedy victory. But, fearing that if he allowed Mr. Key and his party to return immediately they would still have time to warn those defending the Fort, the Admiral told the men that they could not go back to shore until Fort McHenry had been taken and destroyed.

The Americans were permitted to return to their own boat, but there was nothing for Mr. Key and his friends to do but give their word not to attempt to go back to shore.

Now Mr. Key was a volunteer soldier, and we can imagine how unhappy he felt at being made to remain on the "sidelines" during an important battle. His worry was all the greater because his brother-in-law, Judge Joseph Hopper Nicholson, was in charge of the soldiers defending Fort McHenry, and Mr. Key knew how small that force was.

Mr. Key and his companions could see the flag flying over Fort McHenry. All day long they watched it streaming gallantly in the breeze. It is said that the enemy told them to look well at the flag at sunset, warning the three Americans that they would not see it in the morning.

Then the firing began. All night Francis Scott Key heard the loud booming of the guns on the ships and the answering thunder of the cannon from the Fort. There was no sleep for him or his companions that night. The minutes seemed like hours, and the hours seemed like days as they watched and anxiously peered through the darkness.

Whenever a rocket burst high in the air, or a bombshell exploded, the glare gave light enough for them to see the flag still flying over Fort McHenry. Would it be there in the morning? Could the gallant defenders hold out against the enemy?

During the night the firing stopped, only to begin again. Then, after a few hours, the British fire suddenly ceased. Those were trying moments for the watchers, who knew that as long as the firing continued, the Fort was holding its own. What had happened? There were no more flashes of light by which the Fort or the shore could be seen. Even with the help of field glasses, Mr. Key could see nothing through the darkness.

The rest of the night seemed to drag on endlessly as the Americans waited for morning to come. Even when the first faint gray light began to show in the east, an early-morning blanket of fog still hid the shore.

At last the fog lifted, and the men were rewarded, for through the smoke and haze they saw that "the flag was still there." The Star-Spangled Banner over Fort McHenry was floating triumphantly in the breeze. The British attack had failed.

In his wild joy Mr. Key cried out the words that had come to his mind so often during the night: "Oh! say can you see?" Quickly pulling an old envelope out of his pocket, he wrote them down. As the British ships left Chesapeake Bay he continued to write the opening verse of the now famous anthem.

Mr. Key, Mr. Skinner, and their friend Dr. Beanes could now return to shore. On the way back, while the other two men manned the boat, Mr. Key finished the remaining stanzas of his poem. That night at his hotel he called for ink and paper and wrote out a clear copy of the verses as they stand today.

The next day he showed the poem to his brother-in-law, Judge Nicholson, who had been in charge of defending the Fort. So delighted was Judge Nicholson that he rushed over to a printer's and had copies run off at once. These handbills, with the title, "Bombardment of Fort McHenry," were distributed throughout the city.

Stirring words they were, and they fitted a stirring tune. For when Judge Nicholson read Mr. Key's poem, he saw at once that it could be sung to a drinking song then very popular in America. This is not so strange as it may seem, for probably the rhythm of the music had been in Mr. Key's mind all along when he was writing the verses.

That night, in a tavern next to the Holliday Street Theatre in Baltimore, an actor named Ferdinand Durang stood on a chair and sang the new song. There was an immediate outburst of patriotic enthusiasm. The audience went wild with excitement and joy. In a few days the poem was printed in the newspaper, *The Baltimore American*, with the directions that it be sung to the tune of "To Anacreon in Heaven." (This air had come to the United States from England. A song in honor of Anacreon, a lyric poet of Greece, it was probably written by John Stafford Smith, composer to the Chapel Royal in London, about 1775.) Soon all Baltimore was reading the poem and singing the song.

Before long people all over that part of the country were singing it. Other states heard it, and in less than a week it had reached as far as New Orleans—quite a record for those days before the radio and coast-to-coast hook-ups. Before many months, all Americans had taken the song to their hearts.

Mr. Key was thirty-four years old when he wrote his famous song. He was the author of other poems, but none of them was so grand as "The Star-Spangled Banner," which still lives as a lasting monument to his patriotic spirit during a moment of peril to our nation. Though Mr. Key wrote his famous poem on September 14, 1814, it was not until March 3, 1931, one hundred and seventeen years later, that a law was passed making "The Star-Spangled Banner" our official national anthem.

Another permanent tribute to Francis Scott Key is the American flag which is always kept flying over his grave at Frederick, Maryland. This is one of only three places where the flag is permitted to fly both night and day during times of peace.

The Star-Spangled Banner
Service Version

FRANCIS SCOTT KEY

JOHN STAFFORD SMITH

1. O ____ say! can you see, ____ by the dawn's ear - ly
2. On the shore, dim - ly seen ____ thro' the mists of the
3. O ____ thus be it ev - er when ____ free - men shall

light. What so proud - ly we hail'd at the twi - light's last
deep. Where the foe's haugh - ty host in dread si - lence re -
stand Be - tween their loved homes and the war's des - o -

gleam-ing? Whose broad stripes and bright stars, thro' the per - il - ous
pos - es, What is that which the breeze, o'er the tow - er - ing
la - tion! Blest with vic - t'ry and peace, may the heav'n-res - cued

fight, O'er the ram - parts we watch'd, were so gal - lant - ly
steep, As it fit - ful - ly blows, half con - ceals, half dis -
land Praise the Pow'r that hath made and pre - served us a

The other two places are the National Capitol at Washington and the War Memorial at Worcester, Massachusetts.

The "Star-Spangled Banner" that Francis Scott Key saw that memorable night was different from the one we know. It had fifteen stars and fifteen stripes for the fifteen states then in the Union. The design of the American flag later was changed to the thirteen red and white stripes for the thirteen original colonies, with a star for each new state as it joined the Union—forty-eight in all.

The actual flag which inspired Mr. Key to write his poem may still be seen at our National Museum in Washington. It was made by Mrs. Mary Young Pickersgill and her two nieces, in a house still standing on Albemarle Street, Baltimore. The flag is very large, thirty-three feet long and twenty-seven feet wide. There are eleven holes in it made by British shots—a big one in the center from a British bombshell. And a large section in one corner is missing, because one soldier who helped defend the Fort begged, as his dying request, that his body be wrapped in a piece of the "Star-Spangled Banner."

Our national anthem was written by Francis Scott Key out of joy and pride in his country. Today his song has become our song, and every American—boys and girls and grownups—will want to sing it with that same joy and pride, while the Star-Spangled Banner waves, as it always will wave, over "the land of the free and the home of the brave."

Yankee Doodle

The rollicking little song we all know and love as "Yankee Doodle" has caused more quarrels among historians and students of music than any other American song. Nobody knows exactly where the tune comes from.

Some say that it was first sung in England as a nursery rhyme, "Lucy Locket lost her pocket." Others claim that the air originally came from Spain, Hungary, or Holland. Still others insist that it was a German harvest song sung by the reapers.

We do know, though, that the tune of "Yankee Doodle" came to this country in 1755, when the British were at war against the French and the Indians, and that the old air from nobody-knows-where was first used here to poke fun at the American Colonial troops.

The smartly dressed, well-drilled British officers and men, with their red coats and fine guns, gazed with wonder and scorn at their backwoods Yankee allies who came to help them fight the French and Indians. As company after company of the New England and New York troops came into camp, the Britishers, although glad to see them, could not help thinking them a funny sight.

Some of the American Colonial troops (for America was a colony then) had long hair reaching to their shoulders. Some wore wigs, and still others had their hair cropped close. Many wore coonskin caps or mere bags on their heads. Some wore long coats, some wore short; some wore blue and some wore black; and many wore no coats at all. All were ragged and tattered. You can imagine how their lack of skill in marching and their queer clothes made the well-dressed, well-trained British soldiers laugh.

It was to make fun of these ragged Colonial troops that a British army doctor, Dr. Richard Shuckburg, who was a poet and musician as well as a doctor, wrote a song to the old tune from nobody-knows-where. It pleased the well-clad Britishers to mock the Colonials as "Yankee Doodles."

How the term "Yankee" arose is not definitely known, but many people think it comes from the way the Indians pronounced the word "English": Yenglees, Yanglees, Yanklees, and—finally—Yankees. Another story tells us that an early settler in New England fought against a powerful Indian chief named "Yankoo," the Indian word for "Victory." When the settler finally won, the defeated chief Yankoo said, "I no more Yankoo. You now Yankoo." And from that day on, New Englanders and, later, all Americans, were known as "Yankees."

The word "Doodle" comes from an English term meaning "do-little" or "silly."

It might also mean to "tootle" on the flute, regarded by some as a rather foolish occupation. In either case, "doodle" is an insulting word to use in referring to anyone, and that is exactly the way it was first meant to apply to the Americans.

Instead of being angry at the Britishers' joke, however, the Colonial soldiers thoroughly enjoyed both the words and the lively air of the song. "Yankee Doodle" made such a hit that in a short time it was heard in American camps from morning till night.

The Yankees sang and whistled it while they worked, while they marched, and before their camp fires. Its jolly words and jaunty tune seemed to express the spirit of these raw, untrained Colonials. They drilled and marched gaily to its brisk, catchy melody.

The Britishers were delighted at the way their joke had been taken. They would shout with laughter whenever they heard the Colonials sing the song. Then they would mimic and make sport of them. Another favorite pastime of the British troops was to gather in front of the New England churches and sing "Yankee Doodle" as the congregations were singing their psalms and hymns.

"Yankee Doodle" was a song of fun and laughter for more than twenty years—until the Revolutionary War. Then came the Battle of Lexington, when some of those same Americans marched to victory to the strains of the song that had once been used to make fun of them. At Bunker Hill the Americans roared out the now well-known song to the accompaniment of fife and drum. The Britishers' joke turned out to be a sad failure. "Yankee Doodle" became the battle march of the Revolution, and the Colonials made the Britishers dance to its tune.

When Lord Cornwallis surrendered to General Washington at Yorktown in 1781, the British soldiers stacked their guns to the old English air, "The World Turned Upside Down," while the Continental band played the tune that had

Yankee Doodle

Dr. RICHARD SCHUCKBURG · Origin Uncertain

1. Fath'r and I went down to camp, A - long with Cap-tain Good-in';
2. And there we saw a thou-sand men, As rich as Squire Da-vid;
3. And there was Cap-tain Wash-ing-ton Up-on a slap-ping stal-lion,
4. I saw a lit-tle bar-rel, too, The head was made of leath-er;
5. And there I saw a swamp-ing gun, Big as a log of ma-ple,

And there we saw the men and boys As thick as has-ty pud-din'.
And what they wast-ed ev-'ry day, I wish it could be sav-ed.
A - giv-ing or-ders to his men; I guess there was a mil-lion.
They knocked up-on't with lit-tle sticks And called the folks to-geth-er.
Up-on a might-y lit-tle cart, A load for fa-ther's cat-tle.

CHORUS

Yan-kee Doo-dle keep it up, Yan-kee Doo-dle dan-dy,

Mind the mu-sic and the step, And with the girls be hand-y.

6.
And every time they shoot it off
It takes a horn of powder,
And makes a noise like father's gun,
Only a nation louder.

7.
It scared me so I hooked it off,
Nor stopped, as I remember,
Nor turned about till I got home
Locked up in mother's chamber.

become their battle song—"Yankee Doodle."

Later, during the War of 1812, "Yankee Doodle" came in handy, serving another gallant purpose. Aaron Bates kept a lighthouse upon the lonely shore near Scituate, Massachusetts, about twenty-five miles from Boston. One day, while Mr. Bates was working in the fields and his two daughters were in their lighthouse home, a British man-of-war appeared and anchored half a mile off shore. The girls saw a boatload of sailors making their way toward the land, no doubt to raid the country. The two girls acted quickly. Upon the wall of their father's house were hanging the fife and the drum their grandfather had played during the American Revolution. They snatched up the instruments and rushed out to the sand dunes. Hiding there, one blew on the fife, the other beat the drum, each playing as hard and as loudly as she could. And the song they played was none other than "Yankee Doodle." When the British sailors heard the tune, they were sure that American troops were ready and waiting for them. And fearing that they were outnumbered and would be taken by the Yankees if they tried to land, they quickly turned around and rowed back to their ship as fast as they could.

At first there were sixteen stanzas to "Yankee Doodle." But the early Colonials and Americans ever since have delighted in adding more. Today few people know any of the original stanzas, except the first one and the chorus. But every American likes to sing and step along to the song's lilting, stirring rhythm. And "Yankee Doodle" remains a popular national march tune.

As one of its many stanzas puts it:

> *"It suits for feasts, it suits for fun,*
> *And just as well for fighting."*

The house where Dr. Shuckburg wrote "Yankee Doodle" was called the "Yankee Doodle House" during the American Revolution. It was built in 1704 and was presented to the state of New York in 1924 as a museum. You can see it on River Street in Rensselaer, New York.

"Yankee Doodle" is America's first national song. Since it was written, many other patriotic songs have been added to our ever-growing store. But American boys and girls will always remember "Yankee Doodle" not only because of the gay, brisk words and music, but because it is the only song left from the American War of Independence and was the first of the many patriotic songs we love.

Hail, Columbia

George Washington, "the father of our country," inspired two patriotic marches. One, called "General Washington's March," was the most popular band piece in

America from 1770 to about 1780. The other, called "The President's March," later became even more famous as the tune for "Hail, Columbia."

Although for years there was some doubt about who composed it, now we are sure that "The President's March" was written by a man named Philip Phile, who died in Philadelphia in 1793. To understand how the words of this beautiful song came to be written, we must know something of what was going on in our country at that time.

In 1789, the first year Washington was President, the French Revolution broke out. By 1793, France was at war against England and Prussia.

The people of our country did not all favor the same side in this European war. Neighbors, friends, and even families were divided in their feeling about who was right. Some thought our duty was to aid France, because that country had helped the Americans gain their freedom. Others believed in helping England, because the roots of America were in England.

President Washington thought that the just and wise policy was to stay neutral. He wanted us to be friendly with both nations and not to take sides, for he felt that our country was in no condition, after our own War of Independence, to face another war.

Still, Americans continued to disagree. One party, the "Republicans" (who, strangely enough, later became the Democratic Party we know now), under Thomas Jefferson, Samuel Adams, James Madison, and Patrick Henry, favored "Republican France," as she was called. The "Federalists," under the leadership of John Adams and Alexander Hamilton, were inclined to favor England.

The disagreement between the Republicans and the Federalists grew more and more serious, and the gap between the two factions became wider and wider, as Washington's term of office as President neared its end. And when John Adams was elected to succeed Washington as President, he was so afraid that the dispute of the two parties would get the United States into war, that he called George Washington back to take command of the American forces, in case war actually should break out between this country and France. Except just before our Civil War, party feeling has never run so high. Everyone was afraid of what the outcome might be.

At this exciting time a song was born that helped to bring the two factions together.

In Philadelphia, then the capital of our country—and where Congress was in session debating and trying to decide what to do—lived a young lawyer, Joseph Hopkinson. His father, Francis Hopkinson, was a very gifted man and our first native American composer. His son seems to have inherited some of his artistic ability.

For one day a young actor, Mr. Gilbert Fox, came to visit his friend Hopkinson. This Mr. Fox, according to Mr. Hopkinson, had "high talent as a singer" and was about to give a performance for his own benefit at a near-by theater, as actors often did at that time. But he was discouraged by the public's lack of interest in what he had to offer, for everyone was too excited about what Congress was going to do to pay much attention to a mere show. He was sure, however, that if he could get a new patriotic song to fit the popular "President's March," his benefit would be a success.

He called on a Saturday. The performance was scheduled for Monday. His need was great. The poets of his own theatrical troupe had tried to write appropriate words for the music he had selected, but had failed. Joseph Hopkinson said that he would try his best and asked his friend to return the next day, though he warned that he had been given very short notice.

Joseph Hopkinson was as good as his word. Monday morning an advertisement

Hail, Columbia!

JOSEPH HOPKINSON

PHILIP PHILE

1. Hail, Co-lum - bia, hap - py land!__ Hail, ye he - roes! heav'n-born band! Who
2. Im - mor-tal pa - triots! rise once more, De - fend your rights, de - fend your shore; Let
3. Sound, sound the trump of fame!__ Let Wash-ing - ton's great name Ring
4. Be - hold the Chief who now com-mands, Once more to serve his coun-try stands, The

fought and bled in Free-dom's cause, Who fought and bled in Free-dom's cause, And
no rude foe with im - pious hand, Let no rude foe with im - pious hand, In -
thro' the world with loud ap - plause, Ring thro' the world with loud ap - plause; Let
rock on which the storm will beat, The rock on which the storm will beat; But

when the storm of war was gone, En - joyed the peace your val - or won. Let
vade the shrine where sa - cred lies, Of toil and blood the well-earned prize. While
ev - 'ry clime to free-dom dear List - en with a joy-ful ear. With
armed in vir - tue, firm and true, His hopes are fixed on heav'n and you. When

in - de - pend - ence be our boast,__ Ev - er mind-ful what it cost;__
off - 'ring peace, sin - cere and just, In heav'n we place a man - ly trust; That
e - qual skill, with God - like pow'r, He gov - erns in the fear-ful hour Of
hope was sink - ing in dis - may, When gloom ob-scured Co - lum-bia's day, His

CHORUS

Ev - er grate-ful for the prize,__ Let its al - tar reach the skies.
Truth and Jus-tice will pre - vail, And ev'ry scheme of bond-age fail.
hor - rid war; or guides with ease The hap-pier times of hon - est peace. Firm, u - nit-ed
stead-y mind, from chang-es free, Re - solved on death or lib - er - ty.

let us be, Rallying round our lib-er-ty; As a band of brothers joined, Peace and safety we shall find.

appeared in newspapers and on posters throughout the city which said:

. . . By Desire will be presented. . . . A Play, interspersed with Songs in Three Acts, called THE ITALIAN MONK . . . after which an entire New Song (written by a Citizen of Philadelphia) to the tune of "The President's March" will be sung by Mr. Fox, accompanied by the Full Band and the following Grand Chorus:

Firm united let us be,

Rallying around our Liberty,

As a band of brothers join'd

Peace and Safety we shall find!

The announcement packed the house. And when the huge crowd heard the new song, the people went wild with enthusiasm. They demanded it again and again. At last they all stood up and sang the chorus with the actors.

Party lines were forgotten, and supporters of both English and French took the words to their hearts. As they left the theater, they were all singing the chorus together. And by the time they had reached the street, more people gathered around and soon everyone joined in the song.

It is said that President Adams and his cabinet, when they learned what the song was doing to unite the people, attended the theater in a body to hear it for themselves. And when thousands of people gathered in the streets in the evenings to sing the new patriotic song, even the Congressmen found themselves joining in.

Mr. Hopkinson, who later became a United States District Judge, was always modest about the great song he had written and assured people that he never had expected to write anything that would last so long and be sung by so many people.

Mr. Fox, the young actor who first sang "Hail, Columbia," reaped a golden harvest. But he never forgot Joseph Hopkinson, later to become Judge Hopkinson, who in twenty-four hours wrote the song which won his notable success.

"Hail, Columbia" was born at a vital moment in our nation's history. And because it kindled and kept alive the American spirit by lifting it above strife and division of thought, it will always live in the hearts of the American people.

The song's first title was "The Favourite, New Federal Song," but this was soon changed to "Hail, Columbia, Death or Liberty." But the words "Death or Liberty" were dropped, and ever since, the song has been known simply as "Hail, Columbia," from the first words of the first stanza.

For many years "Hail, Columbia" was played by the Navy bands when the flag was lowered at sunset. And until our present national anthem was adopted, European countries generally used "Hail, Columbia" when paying homage to America.

For almost a century the only popular patriotic rivals of "Hail, Columbia" were Francis Scott Key's "The Star-Spangled Banner" and Dr. Samuel F. Smith's "America."

But as "America" was written to the same tune as the British "God Save the King" and "The Star-Spangled Banner" to the old English song, "To Anacreon in Heaven," we should remember "Hail, Columbia" for a very special reason—for both its words and music were products of Americans. In this respect it may be said to be the first wholly American patriotic song.

America

Our national anthem, "The Star-Spangled Banner," written during the attack on Fort McHenry in 1814, is full of the spirit of that battle. The song "America," on the other hand, is hymn-like and peaceful, and does not refer to war in any way.

It was written by a young divinity student in the year 1832. Samuel Francis

Smith was then studying at Andover Academy to become a minister. A friend of his, Lowell Mason, was interested in music; in fact, Mr. Mason was the first man in this country to make music a part of public-school education. Now Mr. Mason had been presented with some German songbooks. And though he himself did not read German, he knew that his friend Samuel Smith did. So he asked Mr. Smith to look over the music books to see if there was any material in them that he might use in his classes. And Mr. Smith agreed to do so. If he found a good tune, he promised either to translate the verse from German into English or to write a new poem to fit the tune.

On a dismal February afternoon Samuel Francis Smith was looking through the books and came across a patriotic song he liked very much. He sang it several times, enjoying its simple, stately melody. As he sang, the thought came to him—why not write a patriotic poem for Americans to sing to that music?

"I seized a scrap of paper from the wastepaper basket," he explained in later years, "and began to write the words that came into my mind.

"In less than half an hour I had written the words for 'My Country, 'Tis of Thee.' I did not know at the time that the tune was the British 'God Save the King.' However, I do not think it a bad idea that we and our cousins [the British] should use the same tune for one of our national songs.

"I did not intend to write a national hymn," continued Dr. Smith, "nor did I ever think that my song, written on the spur of the moment, would become so famous. Little did I realize that what I was writing would mean so much to my people. Such as it is, I am glad to have done something for the cause of American freedom."

Samuel Smith put his poem away in one of the drawers of his desk, and there it remained for several months. He gave Mr. Mason a copy when he returned the songbooks. Then he got interested in other matters and forgot all about his new poem.

On the Fourth of July, Mr. Smith went to a children's celebration in the Park Street Church, Boston. Imagine how overjoyed he must have been when he heard a great chorus of children singing his own song. Mr. Mason, the owner of the music books, had trained the children as a surprise for his friend.

July 4, 1832, is to be remembered as the date when "My Country, 'Tis of Thee," as it was called in the beginning, was first sung in public. Although the audience was pleased with the song, they soon forgot about it, until it came out in a book, *The Boston Academy*, four years later. Its title then was "America, National Hymn." And "America" it has been ever since.

"America" found its way into a few hymnbooks, but as a song to arouse patriotism it did not stir the great mass of people until the Union flag was shot down at Fort Sumter. Then Americans everywhere came to know and love it.

Since then it has been sung more often than any other of our national songs. Its fame is world-wide as a song full of the glory and dignity of the American spirit.

During his long life, Dr. Smith often had the pleasure of hearing both children and grownups sing the song he had written. The country he loved and the flag which it represented were always close to his heart—it is said that the Stars and Stripes waved from the tall pole in front of his house every day.

As to who wrote the tune, no one knows. Like Topsy, it seems as if it "just growed." For years men have looked and searched through records, dug out old manuscripts, compared odd scraps of tune and odd scraps of words. But still no one can say with certainty that at "such-and-such" a time Mr. "So-and-So" wrote the melody which has become one of our great American songs.

The tune of "America" has been used by more countries as a patriotic air than any song ever written. It has been sung in more forms and in more different ways,

America

SAMUEL FRANCIS SMITH

Origin Uncertain

by more civilized nations, than, perhaps, any other single melody. Many stories are told about where the music may have come from, and it has been the subject of endless argument.

The tune, or one like it, was sung long before Christopher Columbus discovered America, and it was known to musicians before the time of Saint Ambrose, who lived in the fourth century.

It is said that the Germans sang the melody before it was taken up by the English. The Germans may have gotten it from the Norsemen, who perhaps heard it sung by the Finns, and the Finns might have learned it from the Huns when they came from Asia into Europe. The Swiss and the French also claim to have their own versions of this same song.

There certainly must be something out of the ordinary in a tune that will strike the hearts of folks from so many races and nations, through so many centuries. Tossed back and forth from country to country, the air at last came to rest among the English-speaking people.

The English version of the song, "God Save The King," is said to have been written by Henry Carey, who also wrote "Sally In Our Alley," and was first sung by the composer at a dinner party in London in 1740, to celebrate a British naval victory. In England it is a prayer for the glory and happiness of the ruler, while in America it is a national song of a great liberty-loving people.

When Franz Josef Haydn, the famous Austrian composer, visited London in 1794, he could not forget the way the Englishmen sang their "God Save The King." Then, too, he noticed that they paid the song as much respect as they did their flag. Upon his return to Austria, Haydn, inspired by "God Save The King," decided to write an anthem for his own country, and the result was the beautiful Austrian national hymn, which was sung from that time until the country was overrun by the Nazis in 1938. This is one of the few times in history when a composer purposely decided to take up his pen and write a national hymn. Patriotic songs that live are seldom made that way.

The tune of our song "America," composed by nobody-knows-who, has lived for hundreds and hundreds of years because people of all nations have loved the music and found it easy to sing.

And our own words, written by the kindly and noble-hearted Dr. Samuel Francis Smith, will live to celebrate American freedom as long as there is a "sweet land of liberty."

Columbia, The Gem of the Ocean

Three of America's favorite songs—"Dixie," "Home, Sweet Home," and "Columbia, The Gem of The Ocean"—were written, at least in part, by actors.

"Columbia, The Gem of The Ocean," like the song "Hail, Columbia," was written by a Philadelphian to oblige a friend. Both were written to help an actor who was to give a benefit performance.

Columbia, the Gem of the Ocean

THOMAS à BECKET

THOMAS à BECKET

1. O Co - lum-bia, the gem of the o - cean, The__ home of the brave and the free,__
2. When war wing'd its wide des-o - la - tion, And__ threatened the land to de - form,__
3. The star-spangled ban-ner bring hith-er, O'er Co - lum-bia's true sons let it wave;__

The shrine of each patriot's de - vo-tion, A __ world of - fers hom-age to thee.
The ark then of freedom's foundation, Co - lum-bia rode safe thro' the storm:
May the wreaths they have won never wither, Nor its stars cease to shine on the brave.

Thy mandates make heroes as - sem-ble, When Lib-er-ty's form stands in view;
With her garlands of vic-t'ry a - round her, When so proud-ly she bore her bold crew,
May the ser-vice u - nit-ed ne'er sev - er, But hold to their col - ors so true;

Thy ban-ners make ty - ran-ny trem-ble When borne by the red, white and blue;
With her flag float-ing proud-ly be - fore us, The boast of the red, white and blue;
The ar - my and na - vy for - ev - er, Three cheers for the red, white and blue;

CHORUS

When borne by the red, white and blue, When borne by the red, white and blue,
The boast of the red, white and blue; The boast of the red, white and blue,
Three cheers for the red, white and blue, Three cheers for the red, white and blue,

Thy ban-ners make tyr - an-ny trem-ble, When borne by the red, white and blue.
With her flag proud-ly float-ing be - fore her, The boast of the red, white and blue.
The ar - my and na - vy for - ev - er, Three cheers for the red, white and blue.

In the autumn of 1843, while Mr. Thomas à Becket was an actor at the Chestnut Street Theater in Philadelphia, he received a call from Mr. David T. Shaw, who was then singing at the Chinese Museum, another theater. Mr. Shaw wanted Mr. à Becket to write a song for him to sing at a benefit performance. He brought with him some patriotic verses that he was considering, but neither he nor Mr. à Becket thought the lines very well written or quite rhythmic enough for singing.

Mr. à Becket promised to write the song Mr. Shaw needed, and the two men then went on to the home of Mr. R. Harford, a friend who lived on Decatur Street. They had been there but a few minutes and were chatting amiably, when Mr. à Becket suddenly seized pencil and paper and began writing feverishly. Not only did he write the first two stanzas of a new song then and there, but at Miss Harford's piano he composed a melody for them. When he returned home that night he added a third stanza, and wrote the introduction and closing measures to the song.

The next day he made a clean copy in ink and gave it to Mr. Shaw, requesting him not to sell or give the new song to anyone, but to keep it for his own use.

"A few weeks afterward I left Philadelphia for New Orleans," Mr. à Becket later wrote in a letter. "Imagine my surprise to see in a music store window a published copy of the song, entitled 'Columbia, The Gem of The Ocean, written, composed and sung by Mr. David T. Shaw and arranged by T. à Becket, Esq.'

"On my return to Philadelphia I waited upon Mr. Willig, the publisher, who told me he had purchased the song from Mr. Shaw. I produced the original copy in pencil and claimed the copyright. Mr. Willig agreed to my claim and told me what he thought of Mr. Shaw for what he had done with my song.

"I then made an arrangement with Mr. T. Osborn of Third Street to publish the song in partnership, and within a week it appeared under its proper title, 'Columbia, The Gem of The Ocean, written and composed by T. à Becket and sung by

D. T. Shaw.' "

Though "Columbia, The Gem of The Ocean" (sometimes called "The Red, White, and Blue") quickly became popular, Mr. à Becket never received the honor due him as the author and composer of one of our best-loved national songs.

It was published in London, "without my authority," Mr. à Becket says, "by T. Williams, of Cheapside, under the title of 'Britannia, The Gem of The Ocean.' " Mr. E. L. Davenport, a prominent English actor of the time, sang the song nightly for several weeks. Furthermore, when Thomas à Becket visited London in 1847, still another unwelcome surprise awaited him, for he found that his song was now claimed as an English composition.

Ill-luck seems to have followed Mr. à Becket and his "Columbia, The Gem of The Ocean." When he returned to America he discovered that his publisher, Mr. Osborn, had failed in business and that the publisher's plates of the song, from which other copies could be printed, had been sold to a dealer in Baltimore.

"And in this way," concludes Mr. à Becket sadly, "it went entirely out of my possession, much to my regret and loss. I never received a penny for my trouble, and got very little credit."

"Columbia, The Gem of The Ocean," was first sung at the Chestnut Street Theater in Philadelphia in 1843, the very same year in which Francis Scott Key died in Baltimore. It belongs to the same general period as "Hail, Columbia," "The Star-Spangled Banner," and "America."

Sometimes called the "Army and Navy Song," because in the third stanza it praises both branches of the service, it is an especially good song to be played when our sea and land forces are taking part in a celebration. It is a favorite at all patriotic gatherings. As one writer has said, "No Fourth of July would be complete without 'Three Cheers for the Red, White, and Blue.' "

Dixie

Long before there were movies and radio comedies, Americans found entertainment at minstrel shows. At these performances the actors came out with their faces blacked, and told stories, danced jigs, cracked jokes, played banjos and other instruments, and sang songs to make people laugh. These minstrel shows were a typically American form of entertainment.

There was always one man who sat in the middle of a semi-circle of minstrels and acted as a master-of-ceremonies. He was called the "middle-man" and was the one who asked the questions that brought forth the funny answers and kept things moving at a lively pace.

The funniest men in the show were the two "end-men" who sat on the outside ends of the semi-circle. Between the middle-man and the end-men there was always a running fire of fun to amuse the audience. The end-men had to tell the funniest stories and dance the fastest jigs, play the banjo, and rattle the bones.

Daniel Decatur Emmett, known as "Jolly" Dan Emmett, was one of the most famous of early American minstrels. He knew the Negro dialects well, and with his face and hands blacked, he could entertain people for hours with his rich store of jokes and songs and dances.

In 1843 "Jolly Dan" organized the Virginia Minstrels, the very first minstrel company on record. With his troupe he traveled all over the United States and was a favorite wherever he went. He even took his company to England, where he was a huge success. But when he returned to the United States, it looked as if his luck had left him, for the troupe was forced to break up, and "Jolly Dan" found out that fame and riches do not always go hand in hand.

In 1858 Dan Emmett joined Dan Bryant's Minstrels in New York. With this company one of "Jolly Dan's" jobs was to make up clever, amusing songs to sing at the close of the show when he walked around the stage. These songs came to be called "walk-arounds." They were so successful, and always brought so much laughter and applause, that the other minstrels spoke of them as "hooray songs."

One Saturday night after the show, as Dan Emmett was leaving the theater, Dan Bryant called him back and said, "Jolly Dan, I want a new 'hooray song' for the show on Monday night. Bring one around to rehearsal on Monday morning."

"Yes, sir," replied Dan Emmett. "This is pretty short notice to make a good one, but you can be sure I'll do my best to please you, Mr. Bryant."

As Dan Emmett walked back to his hotel, a cold wind was blowing and he was chilled through and through. He surely could not be called "Jolly" now. And he was worried about that song he had to write. How could he think of a "hooray song" to make people laugh when he was so cold and so gloomy?

"I wish I was in Dixie," he muttered to himself. In the show business anyone who could get a job in the South—or Dixie-land—during the cold Northern winter thought himself pretty lucky. Once more he said, "I wish I was in Dixie," and as he walked along his steps caught the rhythm of those words.

"Why, that's a good idea for a song!" he exclaimed, and already his heart was lighter. Quickening his pace, he soon reached his hotel, where he immediately sat down to write the words and music as he thought them out. Thus "Dixie," song of the Sunny South, was born on a cold Northern street.

The next day Dan Emmett made a clean copy of the song, and on Monday morning he took it to the rehearsal. To say that it made a hit at the minstrel show that night goes almost without saying. The people cheered and stamped and would not let "Jolly Dan" go until he had sung it again and again.

Dan Emmett's "hooray song" quickly made a name for him. It was taken up at once by other minstrel groups, who sang and danced it in all parts of the country.

In the South it was first heard in New Orleans just before the Civil War began. Late in the year 1860 a big show had been arranged and all the parts and music given out. Each detail had been completed except for selecting a grand march for the chorus to sing at the close of the affair.

One after another various marches and songs were tried, but none seemed to meet the approval of everyone. At last someone suggested "Dixie," and as soon as it had been tried out, the performers enthusiastically agreed that it was just the song

Dixie

DANIEL DECATUR EMMETT

DANIEL DECATUR EMMETT

frost - y morn - in', Look a - way! Look a - way! Look a - way! Dix - ie Land.
bound to trab - ble, Look a - way! Look a - way! Look a - way! Dix - ie Land.

CHORUS

Den I wish I was in Dix - ie, Hoo - ray! Hoo - ray! In

Dix - ie Land, I'll take my stand To lib an' die in

Dix - ie; A - way, A - way, A - way down south in

Dix - ie; A - way, A - way, A - way down south in Dix - ie.

they wanted. That night, when the audience heard it, they were so delighted that the singers had to repeat the song eight times.

After that, "Dixie" was soon being whistled and sung throughout the South—in the streets, in homes, and in concert halls. And when the Civil War began, it was taken to the battlefields and became a favorite in camp and on the march. Soon it came to be known as the official Southern Confederate war song, even though it had been written by a Northerner.

A New Orleans publisher, without asking Dan Emmett, had a new set of words expressing strong Southern feeling written for the melody. This brought no end of trouble to poor Dan Emmett, who was accused by his Northern friends of treason to the Union.

At the close of the war, after the surrender of General Lee in 1865, President Lincoln had "Dixie" played by the band in Washington, saying, "We have captured the Confederate Army; we have also captured the Confederate tune, and both belong to us." Today there is no more South and North, but only the United States of America, and we all sing the same songs together.

After a time, Dan Emmett retired to a little farm at Mt. Vernon, Ohio. He was so modest and quiet that his neighbors could hardly believe that the kindly old man in the cottage at the edge of the town was actually the man who had written "Dixie."

Many people have wondered how Dan Emmett happened to use the word "Dixie." Some think that in his early days as a minstrel "Jolly Dan" heard his fellow-performers call the states south of the Mason and Dixon line "Dixie's land" and wish they were there when the cold winds of the North began to blow.

But others think that the word and the happy thoughts it brought to mind came from the name of a Mr. Dixie, a New York farmer at whose farm runaway slaves always found shelter and kind treatment. And so "Dixie land" is said to have been a

Negro name for a region of peace and plenty where Negroes wished to be.

It is also a fact that the ten-dollar paper currency of a bank in New Orleans was marked "Dix," the French word for "ten." These ten-dollar bills were known as "Dixies," and that may be how the name "Dixie" came to apply to the South.

Northerners tried to keep the "Dixie" tune for themselves, and several poets attempted to write new words. Even Dan Emmett wrote another version, called "Dixie for the Union." But it was too late; "Dixie" belonged to the South, and even though a Northerner did write it, he could never make it a strictly Northern song.

It seems strange that by accident a rollicking "hooray song," with its catchy, jingly rhythm, written for a minstrel-show "walk-around," should have been used to inspire men to go into battle and fight. Yet that is exactly how the song was used by the South during the Civil War. And the quality of this song was such that today it does not seem at all strange that "Dixie" has found a favored place among the enduring songs of the Union.

Maryland, My Maryland

During Civil War days, a great many songs were written by people of both sides, for both North and South wanted songs that would arouse the patriotic spirit of their people.

From the South, one of the first and most fiery war songs was "Maryland, My Maryland." Written by James Ryder Randall, it was set to the music of an old German folk song, "O Tannenbaum," which German children of that time used to sing around the Christmas tree.

The tune was so good that the Northerners wanted to use it too. Soon after the Southern words of "Maryland, My Maryland" were written, the Northerners came out with words of their own and the jolly Christmas melody became a song of war on both sides of the Mason and Dixon line. But it is the Southern song that has lived and that today is sung all over America.

James Ryder Randall, the author of the Southern words, was born in Baltimore, Maryland, January 1, 1830. When he wrote "Maryland, My Maryland," the state of Maryland was one of the "doubtful" states. Although it remained in the Union, it was a slave-holding state, and the feeling for the South was very strong among her people.

A few years before the Civil War began, Mr. Randall had gone to New Orleans, where, at the age of twenty-two, he became a teacher at a near-by college. There, in April, 1861, he read that a regiment of Union soldiers from Massachusetts, passing through Baltimore on their way south to Washington, had been attacked by a mob. A bloody skirmish had followed.

"This news of what had happened in my home city excited me greatly," he wrote in a letter, "and the startling event there upset my mind. I could not rid my thoughts of what I had read in the newspaper. That night when I went to bed I could not sleep, for my nerves were all unstrung.

"I was in a strange, nervous tension. Suddenly at midnight I arose, lit a candle, and went to my desk. Some powerful spirit seemed to move me, and hardly knowing what I was doing, I started to write the song, 'Maryland, My Maryland.'

"The idea seemed to take shape first as music in my brain. It was some wild air that I cannot now recall. The whole poem of eleven stanzas was dashed off rapidly when once begun. It was not composed in cold blood, but under what may be called a fire of my senses and of my mind.

"I was stirred to a desire for some way of linking my name with that of my native state. But I had never dreamed of doing this with one single effort. No one was more surprised than I was at the widespread use of the poem I had been so strangely called to write."

The following morning Mr. Randall read the poem to his students. They were all stirred by his recitation and eager to have him publish his verses. So he gave them to the local paper, the *Delta*, and then thought nothing more about the poem.

"However," Mr. Randall wrote, "other newspapers copied it, until at last it had appeared in every Southern journal. Very soon letters from all parts of the country led me to believe that the poem had made a great hit. Whatever might be the outcome of the Civil War, I knew that the song would win out, long after the fighting had ceased.

"The eyes of both the North and the South were fixed on the Border States, of which Maryland was one. Someone has said that I came at the nick of time, for 'Maryland, My Maryland' seemed to bring the thoughts of my people together. Through my poem, the South seemed to speak. I say this with all modesty."

When a great poem is born at such a time, there is always a desire to put it into song.

Unlike the authors of "Hail, Columbia," and others of our national songs, Mr. Randall had not written "Maryland, My Maryland" to fit a tune already known, and it was left for Miss Jennie Cary of Baltimore to lend the poem musical wings.

"Our house was a meeting place for the Southerners in Baltimore," Jennie's sister Hetty wrote later. "It soon became a marked one, termed by the Union Press 'Headquarters of Rebeldom.'

Maryland, My Maryland

JAMES RYDER RANDALL

German Folk Song

1. The des-pot's heel is on thy shore, Ma-ry-land, my Ma-ry-land! His
2. Hark to an ex-iled son's ap-peal, Ma-ry-land, my Ma-ry-land! My
3. Thou wilt not cow-er in the dust, Ma-ry-land, my Ma-ry-land! Thy

torch is at thy tem-ple door, Ma-ry-land, my Ma-ry-land! A-
Moth-er State, to thee I kneel! Ma-ry-land, my Ma-ry-land! For
gleam-ing sword shall nev-er rust, Ma-ry-land, my Ma-ry-land! Re-

venge the pa-tri-ot-ic gore That flecked the streets of Bal-ti-more, And
life and death, for woe and weal, Thy peer-less chiv-al-ry re-veal, And
mem-ber Car-roll's sa-cred trust, Re-mem-ber How-ard's war-like thrust, And

be the bat-tle queen of yore, Ma-ry-land, my Ma-ry-land.
gird thy beau-teous limbs with steel, Ma-ry-land, my Ma-ry-land.
all thy slumb-'rers with the just, Ma-ry-land, my Ma-ry-land.

"The Glee Club was to hold its meeting in our music room one evening in June. My sister, Miss Jennie Cary, being the only musical member of the family, had charge of the program. With a schoolgirl's eagerness to score a success, she tried to find a new patriotic song for the meeting.

"In vain she looked through her stock of songs and airs, but nothing seemed patriotic enough. I came to the rescue with the suggestion that she should get a tune to fit the words of 'Maryland, My Maryland.' It had been on my lips ever since I saw it in the newspaper. So I got the copy and started to read the verses."

At that time one of the favorite songs among college students both here and abroad was "Lauriger Horatius," a Latin poem set to the old German Christmas tune of "O Tannenbaum." It had been brought into the Cary home first by a Yale student who was a friend of the sisters. When Miss Jennie heard the words of "Maryland, My Maryland," suddenly the college song flashed into her mind. To her joy, the verses fitted the tune perfectly.

That night at the Glee Club meeting, when her rich voice rang out the stanzas, the refrain was taken up and rolled forth from every throat with such a volume of sound that a crowd which had gathered beneath the open windows joined in the chorus.

But the song really became popular when Miss Jennie sang it at a serenade given to the Cary sisters by Maryland troops in General Beauregard's army at Fairfax Court House, Virginia. You can imagine how the soldiers' pride was stirred by the words and melody.

The song was later brought to the Deep South when the two sisters attended a band concert while on a visit to New Orleans. When the band stopped playing, one of the officers said, "Let's hear a woman's voice."

Then Miss Jennie Cary stood up and sang "Maryland, My Maryland." The refrain was taken up by hundreds of soldiers. As the last notes died away, a great shout arose from the men. The original words of "Maryland, My Maryland" were very fiery, and at once became a favorite camp-fire song of the Southern forces.

And it was not only with the armed forces that the song was so popular. No song of the South so shared the glory of "Dixie" as did "Maryland, My Maryland." Guards who protected the city of Baltimore during the Civil War said that in many a home, supposed not to be taking sides, the strains of this ardent and rousing song were often heard at midnight.

Thus did a great song, "Maryland, My Maryland," come from the South, as "The Battle Hymn of the Republic" came from the North. James Russell Lowell, the American poet, said that "Maryland, My Maryland" was the finest poem written during the Civil War. Whether or not one agrees with the great poet's opinion, the song has not only given lasting fame to its author but it has become a favorite song all over the country. After the Civil War was over, "Maryland, My Maryland," like "The Battle Hymn of the Republic," remained to be sung by the entire nation. And today both are among the best-loved songs of American patriotism.

The Battle Cry of Freedom

America, "sweet land of liberty," always has had patriots ready to come to her aid in time of need. When a statesman was needed to lay the foundations of a republic, George Washington was ready. When our Constitution and liberty were threatened, loyal Americans came to her defense.

When it looked as though the Union would be divided and a leader was needed to guide the Republic through the storm, Abraham Lincoln stood at the helm. The first time he called for volunteers to save the nation and its flag, men quickly answered his call. When, however, the President issued his second call for troops in the summer of 1861, there was little response to the appeal. In Chicago the recruiting officers had great difficulty in persuading men to enlist. Clearly something was needed to inspire the citizens and rouse them to action.

George Frederick Root, a Chicago music publisher, who had been writing and publishing songs of his own for some time, felt that a new rallying song would do the trick. Mr. Root thought that such a song, by creating greater patriotic spirit, would help to send more men to the recruiting offices. Deeply concerned by his country's great need, Mr. Root thought about the idea all one day. Toward evening, his spirit seemed to "catch on fire." Words and music crowded into his mind and he could hardly write them down fast enough.

"It seemed as though my pen were being guided," he said afterward. In a very short time he had finished the words and also the music of "The Battle Cry of Freedom," a song that was soon to quicken and stir the hearts of Americans everywhere.

The very next day Jules and Frank Lombard, popular singers of that period, came into Mr. Root's publishing office. A big mass meeting was to be held that day in Court House Square, and the two brothers were looking for something to sing. A message from the President was to be read, and they wanted a brand-new song for their part of the program.

"Here, take a look at this one," said Mr. Root, handing them the song he had just finished. "You must handle it with care, however, as the ink is not yet dry." The Lombards tried the song and were delighted. It was just what they needed.

At noon thousands of people gathered in the square to hear President Lincoln's message to the Union. After the message had been read, the Lombard brothers mounted the Court House steps and began to sing "The Battle Cry of Freedom." Immediately the crowd grew very quiet. And as the two brothers lifted the refrain "The Union forever! Hurrah, boys, hurrah!" in clear trumpet-like tones, the crowd stood spellbound.

After the second verse, a few people began to sing the chorus. Soon more joined in, and the Lombard brothers sang the song over and over until at last everyone was singing it. That meeting turned out to be one of the most moving occasions Chicago had ever known.

And the song had done its job. Even before the last echo had died away, men were rushing over to the recruiting office. So eager were they to enlist that they even scrambled for places in the line.

A few days later the new song was sung at another mass meeting, this time held in Union Square, New York. Excitement ran high and the immense throng was roused to the highest pitch. The "Rallying Song" was sung again and again and proved to be a great force in swelling the ranks of the Union Army in New York, just as it had in Chicago.

"The Battle Cry of Freedom" seemed to travel as if on magic wings. It swept all over the North, into all camps under the Stars and Stripes. Soldiers sang it while they marched and were buoyed up on the battlefield by its martial strains.

From the year 1861 until the close of the war, this rousing song of patriotism was heard everywhere, and the Union cause was greatly aided by its stirring power.

Other songs by Mr. Root also became popular both in the North and the South. "Tramp, Tramp, Tramp, the Boys Are Marching," "The Vacant Chair," and "Just Before the Battle, Mother," were sung in homes as well as in camps.

More than any other composer of Civil War days, Mr. Root seemed to know

The Battle Cry of Freedom

GEORGE FREDERICK ROOT

GEORGE FREDERICK ROOT

1. Yes, we'll ral - ly round the flag, boys, we'll ral - ly once a - gain,
2. We are spring - ing to the call of our broth - ers gone be - fore,

Shout-ing the bat-tle cry of Free-dom; We will ral - ly from the hill - side, we'll
Shout-ing the bat-tle cry of Free-dom; And we'll fill the va - cant ranks with a

gath - er from the plain, Shout-ing the bat - tle cry of Free - dom!
mil - lion free men more, Shout-ing the bat - tle cry of Free - dom!

CHORUS

It's Free-dom for-ev-er, Hur - rah, boys, Hurrah! Down with the shackle and up with the star!

While we ral-ly round the flag, boys, we'll rally once a-gain, Shouting the battle cry of Free-dom!

just what kind of songs were needed. His songs not only moved men to enlist but also gave the soldiers courage to go into battle. To all who sang or heard them they brought good cheer. They helped keep alive a spirit of hope and they caused many thousands of men to rally round and follow the flag, for they always touched the hearts of men.

George Frederick Root played an important part in the struggle for human liberty. Through his songs and especially "The Battle Cry of Freedom," Mr. Root had as great an influence during the dark days of the Civil War as many men who were officially listed as heroes.

President Lincoln himself wrote Mr. Root and thanked him for the great service he had done his country. The President said that these songs of patriotism, as much as anything else, had helped in winning the Civil War.

The Battle Hymn of the Republic

When the Civil War broke out, there was need for a patriotic hymn to express the martial spirit of the times. A new song was wanted, one that would be a great battle hymn, yet one that would be suitable in time of peace as well.

To find such a hymn, a group of men got together and offered a prize of two hundred and fifty dollars for the best words, and another two hundred and fifty dollars for the best melody.

Poets and musicians all over the North immediately set to work, and in three months' time twelve hundred songs were sent in. But not one of them was what the group of men offering the prizes thought a real patriotic song should be.

Unfortunately, a national hymn seems to be one of those things that cannot be made to order. As Dr. Smith, who wrote "America," said: "A noble song like 'My Country, 'Tis of Thee' is not written, it just comes." Great songs rise from hearts overflowing with noble feelings. The making of a national song is a happy accident, and its author often does not suspect that he is giving the world something that may last forever. Perhaps that is why the twelve hundred songs written for the prize failed. Of all those songs not one of them is ever heard or sung today. Because they were not truly inspired, they could not appeal to the hearts of people everywhere.

However, one person was ready at this time to give the country the hymn so greatly needed. It was Julia Ward Howe who answered her country's call and presented to the nation a song that will never be forgotten: "The Battle Hymn of the Republic."

Mrs. Howe had written many articles against slavery for *The Commonwealth,* a Boston newspaper of which her husband, Dr. Samuel G. Howe, was editor. Even as a child Mrs. Howe had been gifted and had shown a fine talent for writing. During her lifetime she wrote many books, but the work which brought her the most lasting fame was the song, "The Battle Hymn of the Republic."

In December of 1861 Mrs. Howe started on a train journey from Boston to Washington, for her husband was then a medical adviser to the Army. She herself has told us about the troops she saw, about the train rushing through the darkness, and the many camp fires along the tracks where soldiers were on guard. When she arrived in the city, she saw officers hurrying to and fro, and heard nothing but talk about the war and the next battle.

The gallop of horsemen, the tramp of men, the noise of drum, fife, and bugle filled the air. All around were sounds of war. Her heart was heavy with sorrow for the bloodshed that was to come.

The next day Mrs. Howe and some friends drove out to the Army camp to see the soldiers parade. Suddenly the enemy attacked, and there was sharp fighting, but at last the enemy was driven off. The visitors were not harmed, but the trip back to Washington was a very slow one, for the road was blocked by marching soldiers.

As the carriage crept along, Mrs. Howe began to sing Army songs, and soon her friends joined in. Among the songs they sang, much to the delight of the soldiers who were crowded around her carriage, was the old favorite, "John Brown's Body." Before long the soldiers, too, took up the stirring refrain of "Glory, Hallelujah," and the air was filled with the sound of singing, marching men.

Now "John Brown's Body" was not a new song. Composed around 1856 by William Steffe, a writer of popular Sunday School songs, it was first sung as a hymn near Charleston, South Carolina, with the words:

> "*Say, brothers, will you meet us*
>
> "*On Canaan's happy shore?*"

It was popular in both white and Negro churches, and in Army posts. One Army post, stationed at Boston Harbor, used to sing it and make up their own verses for it, most of them funny.

One member of this Boston regiment was named John Brown, just like the famous John Brown who not so long before had made his brave stand against slavery. To tease their own John Brown, the soldiers of this regiment made up verses about him to the hymn tune in which they sang:

> "*John Brown's body lies a-mouldering in the grave,*
>
> "*His soul goes marching on.*"

And they kept the "Glory, Hallelujah" chorus. The song was taken up by other regiments also and became a great favorite. This was the song Mrs. Howe sang and heard the troops sing that day near Washington.

Dr. Clarke, Mrs. Howe's pastor, who was one of the party, said, "Mrs. Howe, why don't you write some good words for that stirring tune?"

"I am afraid," replied Mrs. Howe, "that I could never write a poem worthy of such a song, or worthy of these times."

"However," she tells us, "just to please the dear old man, I promised to try."

That night when she went to bed she could not sleep; the excitement of the day had been too much for her. She could still hear the thump-thump-thump of the soldiers' feet and their voices singing endlessly about John Brown's soul marching on. Try as she would, she could not drive the tune from her mind.

As she lay there, new words began coming to her, and for the next few hours she found herself singing them quietly to the old "John Brown" tune. Line after line came into her mind, till at last she had thought out five complete stanzas. "I felt," she wrote later, "that I must write those words down before I would forget them. I was afraid that if I went to sleep they might not come back to me in the morning.

"I sprang out of bed and felt around in the dark to find a bit of paper and the stump of a pencil which I remembered to have had the evening before. I was used to writing in a room that had been darkened when putting my children to sleep.

"So I began to write the lines of the poem, and in a little while had the five stanzas of the complete song as I had thought it out. Then I went back to bed."

As she dropped off to sleep she thought to herself, "I like this better than anything I have ever written."

A day or two later she showed her verses to Dr. Clarke, and he was greatly pleased with them. After her return to Boston she took the poem to Mr. James T.

Fields, editor of *The Atlantic Monthly*, who thought it so good that he promised to print it in the magazine.

The poem was first printed in February, 1862, with a title chosen by Mr. Fields: "The Battle Hymn of the Republic." Somehow or other, Mrs. Howe's name was left out, so at first no one knew who had written the verses. A few days later Mrs. Howe received the sum of five dollars for the lines that were to become famous all over the world.

Mrs. Howe must have been especially pleased to have the poem printed in *The Atlantic Monthly*, for when the famous American poet James Russell Lowell had been editor of that magazine, he had refused to publish a poem she had sent in, saying he thought no woman could write a poem. Although that gentleman wrote many verses, none of them is as well known and probably none will live so long as Mrs. Howe's "Mine eyes have seen the glory of the coming of the Lord."

Mrs. Howe was too busy reading war news to pay much attention to her poem, and so she did not know how fast her song was making its way nor what a strong hold it was taking on American hearts. People began to ask the name of the author, and great was their surprise when they found out that the fiery words were the work of a sweet, gentle woman. Soon Mrs. Howe's name became known throughout the land. Newspapers everywhere were now printing "The Battle Hymn of the Republic."

It was the poem of the hour. The Union armies took it up as the great marching song of the North. It was a favorite in the soldiers' camps and in homes, and the words were on everyone's lips. The swing of the familiar "John Brown" tune helped the song to spread to the far corners of the earth, for it is one of the best marching melodies ever written.

There is a moving story showing how much the song meant to a group of men

The Battle Hymn of the Republic

JULIA WARD HOWE

Origin Uncertain

1. Mine eyes have seen the glo - ry of the com - ing of the Lord; He is
2. I have seen Him in the watchfires of a hun - dred cir - cling camps, They have
3. I have read a fi - ery gos - pel writ in bur - nished rows of steel: "As ye
4. He has sound - ed forth the trum - pet that shall nev - er call re - treat; He is
5. In the beau - ty of the lil - ies Christ was born a - cross the sea, With a

tramp - ling out the vint - age where the grapes of wrath are stored; He hath
build - ed Him an al - tar in the eve - ning dews and damps; I can
deal with My con - tem - ners, so with you My grace shall deal." Let the
sift - ing out the hearts of men be - fore His judg - ment seat. Oh, be
glo - ry in His bos - om that trans - fig - ures you and me; As He

loosed the fate - ful light - ning of His ter - ri - ble swift sword: His truth is marching on.
read His righteous sentence by the dim and flar - ing lamps: His day is marching on.
He - ro born of wom - an crush the ser - pent with His heel, Since God is marching on.
swift, my soul, to an - swer Him! be ju - bi - lant my feet! Our God is marching on.
died to make men ho - ly, let us die to make men free, While God is marching on.

CHORUS

Glo - ry, glo - ry, hal - le - lu - jah! Glo - ry, glo - ry, hal - le - lu - jah!

Glo - ry, glo - ry, hal - le - lu - jah! His truth is march - ing on.

during the Civil War. Fighting Chaplain McCabe of an Ohio regiment had read Julia Ward Howe's poem in *The Atlantic Monthly* and had learned it by heart. Some time later he was captured by the Confederates and sent to prison. When the news of the Northern victory at Gettysburg came to the prisoners, Chaplain McCabe stood up and sang the "Battle Hymn of the Republic," and all the prisoners sang with him. After he was free, McCabe told this story to a large audience in Washington, among whom was President Lincoln. When he got to the part about the prisoners singing the song, the Chaplain again sang it there on the stage. As the last chorus came to a close, President Lincoln was so moved, that, with tears streaming down his cheeks, he cried out, "Sing it again!"

When she was an old lady, Mrs. Howe said, "My poem did some service in the Civil War. I wish very much that it may do good service in the Peace, which I pray God may never more be broken."

Mrs. Howe's wish has come true. For "The Battle Hymn of the Republic" is one of the songs of Civil War days that may be sung by North, South, East, and West. Although it was written by a Northerner, it does not speak of boundary lines. Mrs. Howe put into her poem the spirit of all Americans, everywhere.

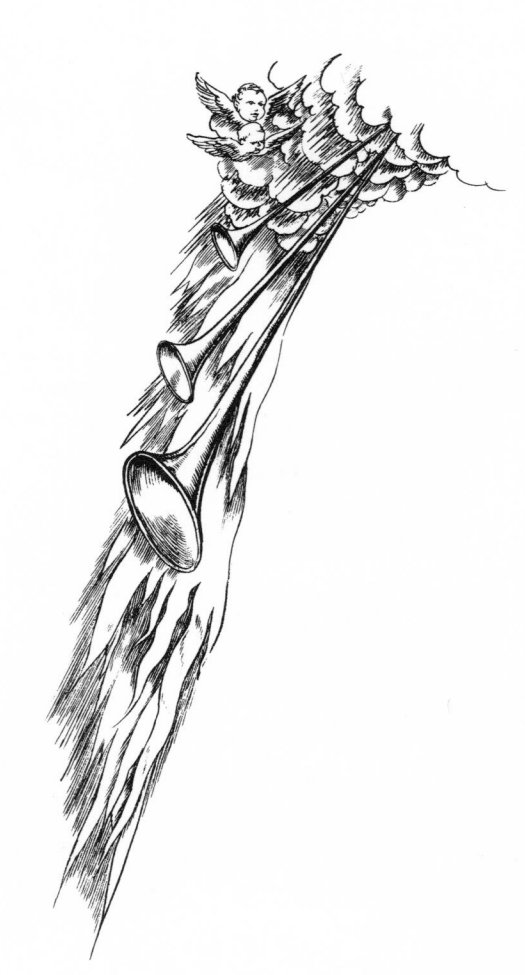

America, The Beautiful

The story of "America, The Beautiful" is quite different from that of "Dixie" or "The Battle Hymn of the Republic" and other of our patriotic songs born of the emotions and excitement of a war.

Miss Katherine Lee Bates, a New England-born professor of English at Wellesley College, in 1893 did what all good Easterners were then doing: she visited the great Chicago World's Fair to see with her own eyes what progress the West had been making. After seeing the Fair, she went to Colorado Springs, Colorado, where she was to teach school during the summer.

When summer school was over, she and some of the other Eastern teachers decided to take a mountain trip and go to the top of Colorado's famous Pikes Peak.

"Those of us who were not young enough to climb on foot," she wrote later, "nor brave enough to ride a donkey, got aboard the prairie wagon. This was an old springless wagon, painted on each side with 'Pikes Peak or Bust,' and drawn first by horses, later by mules."

At last, after a long, bumpy ride, they reached the summit of the mountain. The day was clear and bright, and for miles in every direction Miss Bates could see deep blue and purple mountains, green valleys, vast amber prairies stretching out into the distance. It was that beautiful, awe-inspiring view of the spaciousness and majesty of her own country that moved Miss Bates to write the first stanza of her now famous poem.

She had hoped to spend at least half an hour on the summit, but two of the group became so faint from the high, thin air that the whole party was bundled into the wagon again and started down. Her stay on the peak lasted scarcely more than a moment, yet it was long enough for Miss Bates to have seen and felt what she put into her poem.

Not only did she write of the wide vista she had seen from that mountain top, but into "America, The Beautiful" she put her dream of a still greater and nobler America.

"It was then and there," Miss Bates afterward wrote, "as I was looking out over the sea-like expanse of fertile country spreading so far away under those ample skies, that the opening line of the hymn floated into my mind.

"The trip down the trail found us all very quiet; we were all rather overcome with awe at the breathtaking sight. When I reached my hotel, I was still under the spell of the scene. I sat down and quickly wrote the rest of the poem.

"Upon my return to Wellesley, work soon took all of my time and thought. The notebook containing my poem was laid aside, and I completely forgot it until two summers later. I then made a copy of the poem and sent it to a magazine [*The Congregationalist*], and 'America, The Beautiful' first came out in print on July 4, 1895."

It was read by people all over the country. Then came a flood of letters from every part of the nation thanking and praising Miss Bates for her poem. Thousands said that she had put into words what every true American felt in his heart.

The original poem, as it came into being on the top of Pikes Peak, was written for grownups to read. But when Miss Bates found out how interested in it so many people were, she wrote simpler words so that every boy and girl would be able to understand them. These were published in a Boston newspaper on November 19, 1904.

When "America, The Beautiful" first appeared as a poem, many people felt that it would make a splendid song. Composers from all parts of the country asked to be allowed to set it to music, and almost one hundred different tunes and melodies were sent in. But not one of them seemed entirely suitable.

At last Miss Bates decided that it would be better to set her poem to a melody that most people already knew, so that the song would be easier for large crowds to sing. So she began looking among old and familiar hymn tunes.

The hymn she finally picked out was called "Materna," which is the Latin word

America, the Beautiful

KATHERINE LEE BATES

SAMUEL A. WARD

for "motherly." At that time this tune, by Samuel A. Ward, was being sung in many churches with the words "O, Mother Dear, Jerusalem." Today, however, almost every church hymnal and all school songbooks use Mr. Ward's tune "Materna" for "America, The Beautiful."

Mr. Ward will be remembered with pleasure and gratitude for his hymn tune. And Miss Bates' poem will live the longer in the memories of Americans because of the stately melody she chose for it.

The song, "America, The Beautiful" has made its way around the world. In Australia the people sing it with the word "America" changed to "Australia." In Canada it is sung with the refrain "Canada, The Beautiful," and in Mexico with the words "Mi Mejico" in the refrain.

"America, The Beautiful" was chosen by the National Women's Clubs as its official song and is sung at all their meetings. Some years ago they thought that perhaps a better tune could be found for it. So the Clubs offered a prize of five hundred dollars to the composer who could write a more suitable musical setting.

Again hundreds of tunes were sent in, but not one of them seemed to fit the words as well as the one originally chosen by Miss Bates. No one won the prize, and we are happy that the old melody is still used today.

For many years the subject of an official national anthem for the United States of America was debated. But for some reason or other people could never agree, and the choice was put off for a long time. At one time when the matter came up before Congress, many Americans felt that "America, The Beautiful" should be selected.

The author once said that the reason her hymn gained such favor with the American people was because Americans are at heart idealists with a deep and abiding faith in human brotherhood. "That is why," she wrote, "I used the word brotherhood so many times in my song."

The noble words of "America, The Beautiful" lift the hearts and minds of Americans as few songs have power to do. The plea for brotherhood and a richer, freer national life breathes through its every line and inspires us to work for that great and ennobling cause.